M000121964

Weather Bear's
Clever Calendar
Calendar & Weather Clip Art for
Classroom & Home

Created & Designed by Dianne J. Hook

ISBN 1-59441-190-5

Contents

Credits

Illustrator: Dianne J. Hook
Project Director: Jennifer Weaver-Spencer
Content Design: Sherrill B. Flora, Jennifer Weaver-Spencer
Cover Production: Annette Hollister-Papp

Clip Art Assembly Basics

Here are some suggestions as you complete projects using clip art from this book.

Tools

Putting together the right tools will make your project go more smoothly and look better in the end. A good **copy machine** is a must. It's worth the extra effort to make sure your school or copy shop has machines that make clean copies. You will also need a bottle of white **paper correction fluid**, a fine-tip **black marker** to combine designs and add your own art to the project, **rubber cement** to mount the design onto your paper during the layout stage of your project, and **scissors** for cutting apart the designs you choose. Optional tools to help create a professional-looking project are a **nonreproducible blue pencil**, to make marks that will not show up on copies; a **proportion scale**, to help you determine the size of the reduction or enlargement necessary to fit your paper; and **blue grid paper** for laying out the project with straight lines.

Assembly Steps

1. Choose the design or designs for the project that you will be making.

2. Make copies of each design before cutting. Use this book as a resource, do not cut images directly from the book.

3. Cut out the designs from your copies, then arrange and place the them on your paper. Blue grid paper can be used to guide straight lines and is usually not visible when copied. A light table or overhead projector can also help with the layout of your page. When you are satisfied with your layout, tape or glue designs in place and make a clean copy.

4. Add illustrations and finishing touches to your layout to make it unique.

5. Make your final copies of the page. Easy!

Weather and Calendar Basics

Use the calendar and weather clip art in this book to create a weather and calendar center at the front of the classroom. Each morning, display the correct weather and matching bear, and point out the new date on the monthly calendar. You can also place the blank calendar, numbers, cover-ups, etc., at a center and have children create their own calendars for the month.

Hints

✦ Keep a ¼-inch margin on all edges of your paper.
✦ If the edges of the cutout pieces are visible on your copies, lighten the copy machine one notch or use correction fluid on one copy and then use it to make the final copies.
✦ Removable tape is great for creating layouts if you will be using the design more than once.

Using Clip Art on CD

All clip art presented in this book is available on the enclosed CD. If desired, the images can be easily layered to create calendars, weather displays, etc. The CD is Mac and PC compatible.

Have fun! You can become an artist and create wonderful projects for your class with the help of this book!

4

Fall

Spring

Spring

Summer

Sunscreen

Sunscreen

Summer

Sunscreen

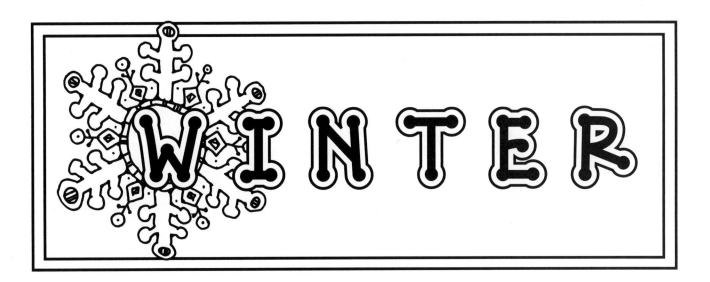

14

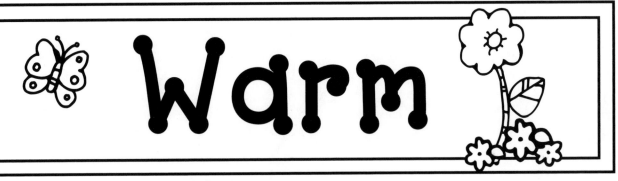

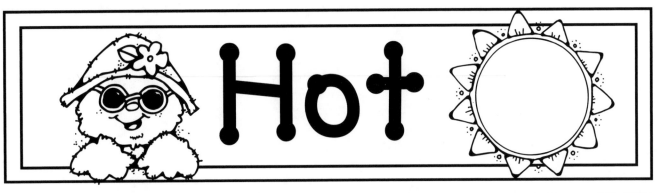

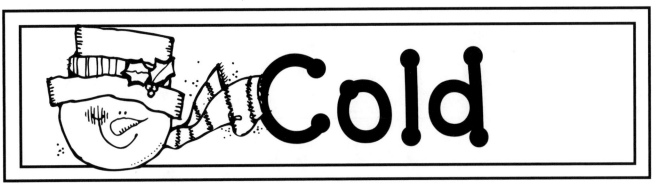

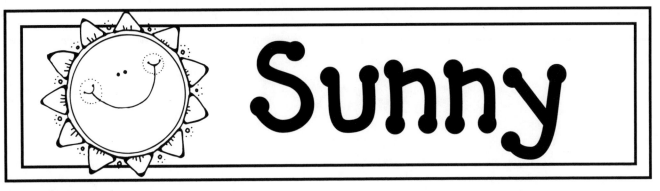

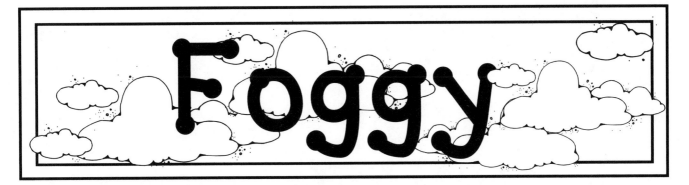

Leaf Border

Beach Border

25

Rain Border

2b

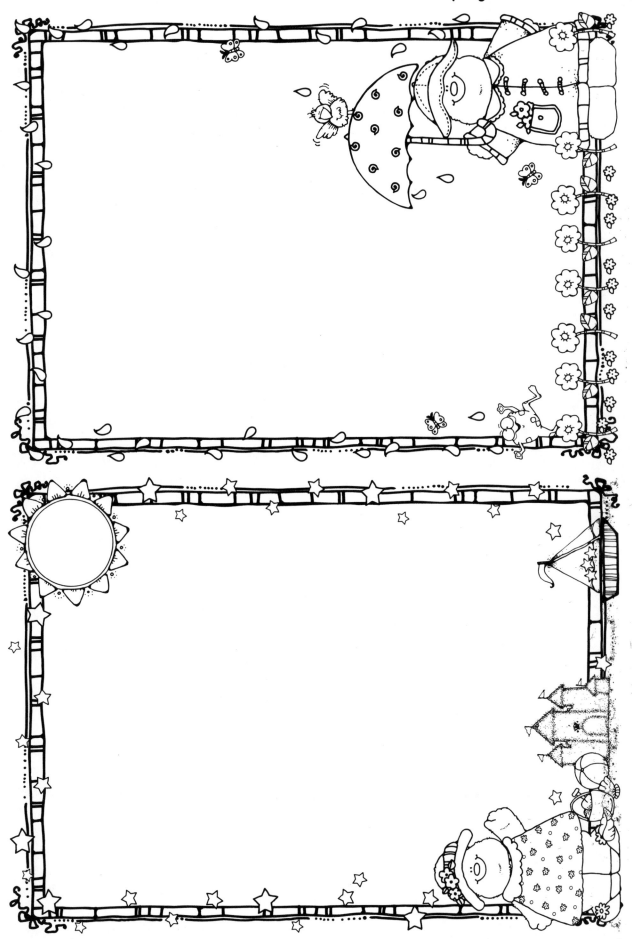

Sunday Sun.	Monday Mon.	Tuesday Tues.	Wednesday Wed.	Thursday Thurs.	Friday Fri.	Saturday Sat.

Bear Header

30

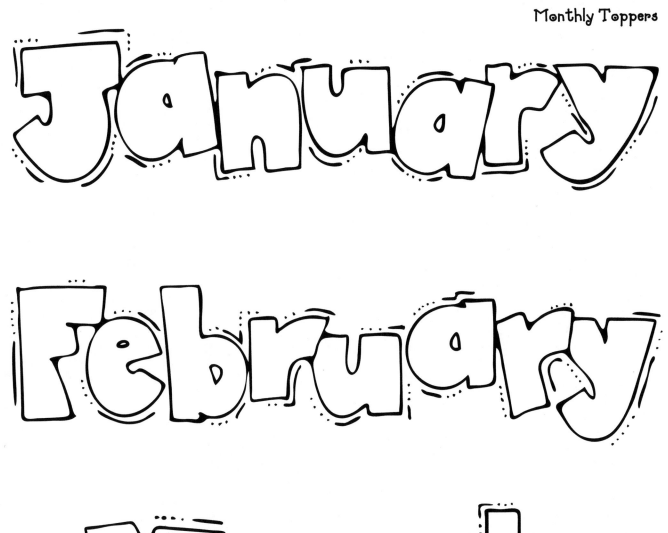

1 2 3 4 5 6 7
8 9 10 11 12
13 14 15 16
17 18 19 20
21 22 23 24
25 26 27 28
29 30 31 0

38

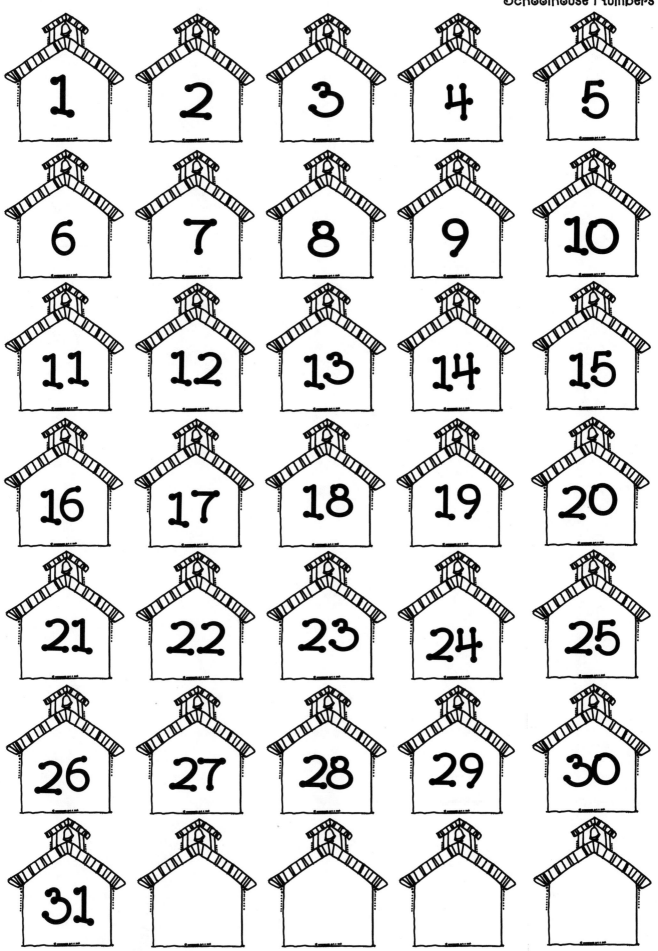

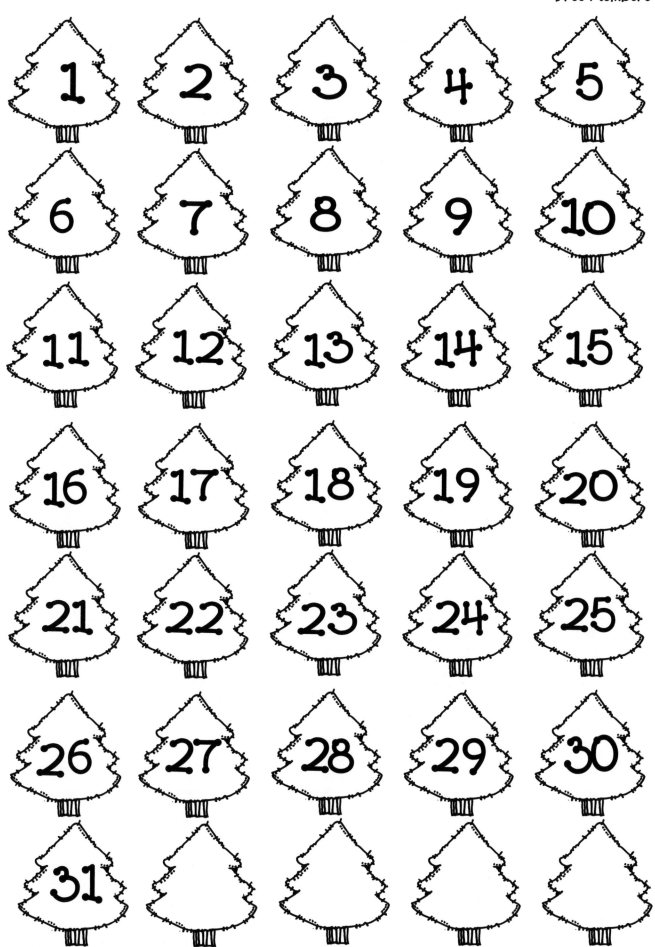

Special Day!

Homework Due Today

FieldTrip!

Don't Forget

Happy Birthday!

Parent Reminder

Picture Day!

Lunch Helpers

Teacher Reminder!

School's Out!

Quiz Today

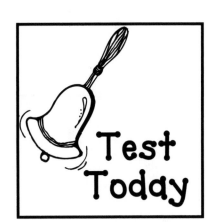

Test Today

Monday

Tuesday

Wednesday

Thursday

Friday

Saturday

Sunday

January

February

March

April

May

June

July

August

September

October

November

December

Winter Break

Spring Break

Fall Break

Christmas

Easter

St. Patrick's Day

Thanksgiving

Hanukkah

Kwanzaa

Valentine's Day

Halloween

New Year's Day

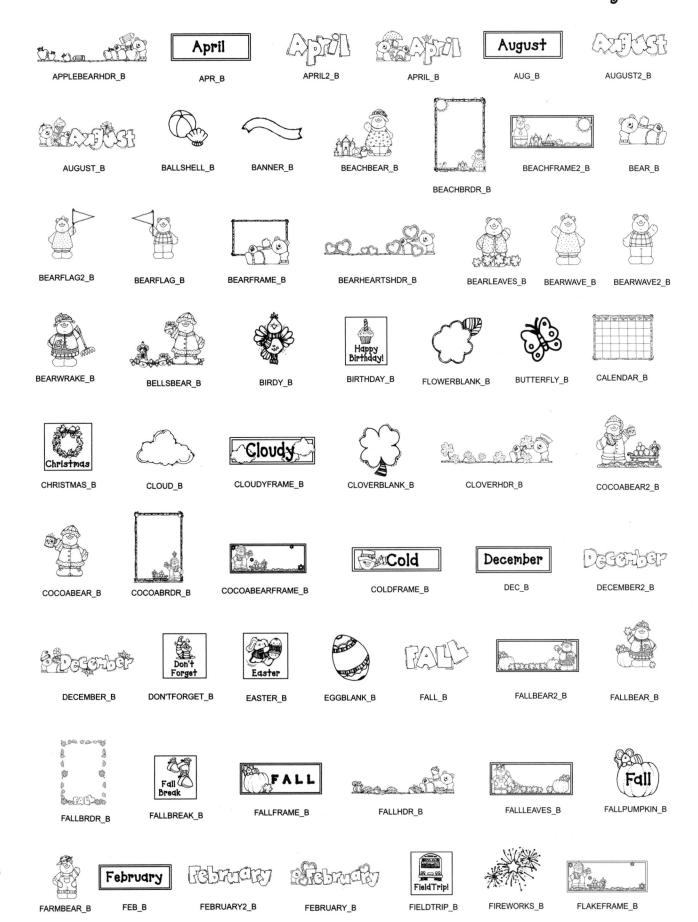

APPLEBEARHDR_B

APR_B

APRIL2_B

APRIL_B

AUG_B

AUGUST2_B

AUGUST_B

BALLSHELL_B

BANNER_B

BEACHBEAR_B

BEACHFRAME2_B

BEAR_B

BEACHBRDR_B

BEARFLAG2_B

BEARFLAG_B

BEARFRAME_B

BEARHEARTSHDR_B

BEARLEAVES_B

BEARWAVE_B

BEARWAVE2_B

BEARWRAKE_B

BELLSBEAR_B

BIRDY_B

BIRTHDAY_B

FLOWERBLANK_B

BUTTERFLY_B

CALENDAR_B

CHRISTMAS_B

CLOUD_B

CLOUDYFRAME_B

CLOVERBLANK_B

CLOVERHDR_B

COCOABEAR2_B

COCOABEAR_B

COCOABRDR_B

COCOABEARFRAME_B

COLDFRAME_B

DEC_B

DECEMBER2_B

DECEMBER_B

DON'TFORGET_B

EASTER_B

EGGBLANK_B

FALL_B

FALLBEAR2_B

FALLBEAR_B

FALLBRDR_B

FALLBREAK_B

FALLFRAME_B

FALLHDR_B

FALLLEAVES_B

FALLPUMPKIN_B

FARMBEAR_B

FEB_B

FEBRUARY2_B

FEBRUARY_B

FIELDTRIP_B

FIREWORKS_B

FLAKEFRAME_B

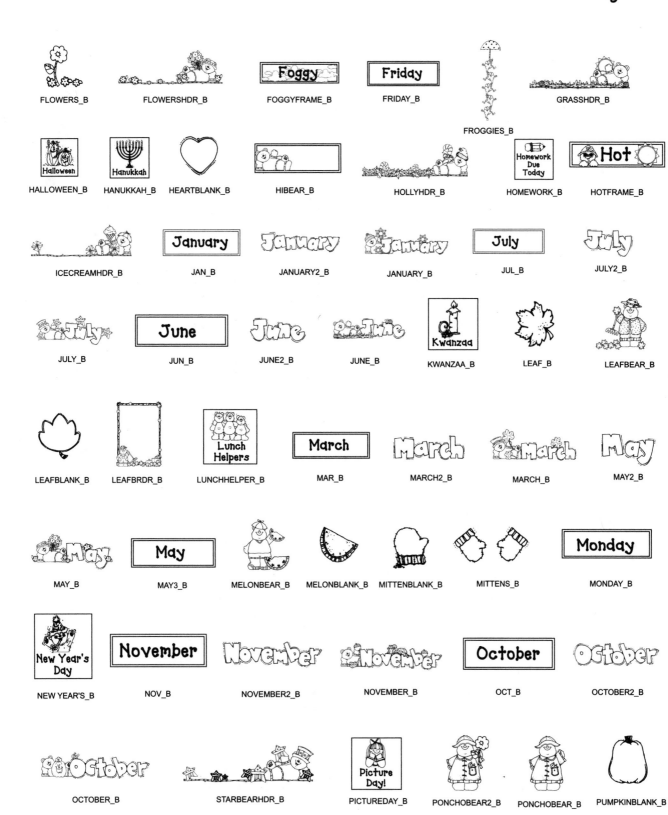

FLOWERS_B   FLOWERSHDR_B   FOGGYFRAME_B   FRIDAY_B   GRASSHDR_B

FROGGIES_B

HALLOWEEN_B   HANUKKAH_B   HEARTBLANK_B   HIBEAR_B   HOLLYHDR_B   HOMEWORK_B   HOTFRAME_B

ICECREAMHDR_B   JAN_B   JANUARY2_B   JANUARY_B   JUL_B   JULY2_B

JULY_B   JUN_B   JUNE2_B   JUNE_B   KWANZAA_B   LEAF_B   LEAFBEAR_B

LEAFBLANK_B   LEAFBRDR_B   LUNCHHELPER_B   MAR_B   MARCH2_B   MARCH_B   MAY2_B

MAY_B   MAY3_B   MELONBEAR_B   MELONBLANK_B   MITTENBLANK_B   MITTENS_B   MONDAY_B

NEW YEAR'S_B   NOV_B   NOVEMBER2_B   NOVEMBER_B   OCT_B   OCTOBER2_B

OCTOBER_B   STARBEARHDR_B   PICTUREDAY_B   PONCHOBEAR2_B   PONCHOBEAR_B   PUMPKINBLANK_B

PUMPKINHDR_B   PUMPKINS_B   QUIZ_B   RAINBEAR_B   RAINBEARHDR_B   RAINBRDR_B

RAINFRAME_B

RAINYBEAR_B

RAINYFRAME_B

RAINYFRAME2_B

REMINDER_B

REMINDER2_B

SAILBEAR_B

SAILBOAT_B

SANDCASTLE_B

SANDPAIL_B

SATURDAY_B

SCHOOLBLANK_B

SCHOOLSOUT_B

SEPT_B

SEPTEMBER_B

SEPTEMBER2_B

SNOWBEARHDR_B

SNOWFLAKE_B

SNOWMAN_B

SNOWMAN2_B

SNOWYFRAME_B

SPECIALDAY_B

SPRING_B

SPRINGBRDR_B

SPRINGBREAK_B

SPRINGCLOUD_B

SPRINGFRAME_B

SQUARE_B

STARBEAR_B

STARBLANK_B

STPATRICK_B

SUMMER_B

SUMMERBRDR_B

SUMMERFRAME_B

SUMMERSUN_B

SUNBEAR_B

SUNBLANK_B

SUNDAY_B

SUNNYFRAME_B

SUNSCREEN_B

TEST_B

THANKSGIVING_B

THURSDAY_B

TREEBLANK_B

TUESDAY_B

UMBRELLABEAR_B

VALENTINE_B

WARMFRAME_B

WEATHERFRAME_B

WEDNESDAY_B

WINDYFRAME_B

WINTER_B

WINTERBANNER_B

WINTERBEAR_B

WINTERBRDR_B

WINTERBREAK_B

WINTERFRAME_B

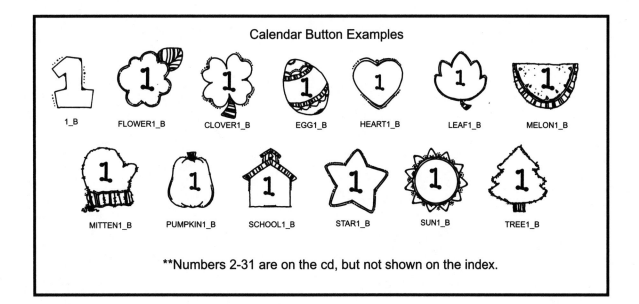

Calendar Button Examples

1_B   FLOWER1_B   CLOVER1_B   EGG1_B   HEART1_B   LEAF1_B   MELON1_B

MITTEN1_B   PUMPKIN1_B   SCHOOL1_B   STAR1_B   SUN1_B   TREE1_B

**Numbers 2-31 are on the cd, but not shown on the index.